# Jacksonville Jaguars

BY
ZACH WYNER

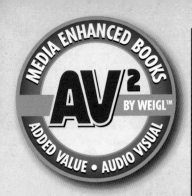

AV² provides enriched content that supplements and complements this book. Weigl's AV² books strive to create inspired learning and engage young minds in a total learning experience.

## Your AV² Media Enhanced books come alive with...

**Audio**
Listen to sections of the book read aloud.

**Key Words**
Study vocabulary, and complete a matching word activity.

**Video**
Watch informative video clips.

**Quizzes**
Test your knowledge.

**Embedded Weblinks**
Gain additional information for research.

**Slide Show**
View images and captions, and prepare a presentation.

Go to www.av2books.com, and enter this book's unique code.

**BOOK CODE**

T822651

**Try This!**
Complete activities and hands-on experiments.

## ... and much, much more!

**AV² by Weigl** brings you media enhanced books that support active learning.

Published by AV² by Weigl
350 5th Avenue, 59th Floor
New York, NY 10118
Websites: www.av2books.com          www.weigl.com

Library of Congress Control Number: 2014931150

ISBN 978-1-4896-0838-3 (hardcover)
ISBN 978-1-4896-0840-6 (single-user eBook)
ISBN 978-1-4896-0841-3 (multi-user eBook)

Printed in the United States of America in North Mankato, Minnesota
1 2 3 4 5 6 7 8 9 0  18 17 16 15 14

052014
WEP150314

Project Coordinator  Aaron Carr
Art Director  Terry Paulhus

Photo Credits
Every reasonable effort has been made to trace ownership and to obtain permission to reprint copyright material. The publishers would be pleased to have any errors or omissions brought to their attention so that they may be corrected in subsequent printings.

Weigl acknowledges Getty Images as its primary image supplier for this title.

# INSIDE THE NFL

# Jacksonville Jaguars

## CONTENTS

# Introduction

The city of Jacksonville, Florida, was a football town long before the Jaguars arrived. The city has hosted the **annual** Florida vs. Georgia Football Classic since 1933. It has also hosted the **Gator Bowl** since 1946. Jacksonville was home to two football teams in the 1970s and 1980s, the Jacksonville Sharks of the World Football League (WFL) and the Jacksonville Bulls of the United States Football League (USFL). Neither of these leagues survived, but the support the local teams enjoyed caught the attention of National Football League (NFL) owners.

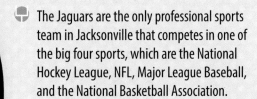 The Jaguars are the only professional sports team in Jacksonville that competes in one of the big four sports, which are the National Hockey League, NFL, Major League Baseball, and the National Basketball Association.

In 1993, the NFL announced the city of Charlotte, North Carolina, was the winner of the first of two **expansion teams**. The people of Jacksonville, St. Louis, Baltimore, and Memphis held their collective breath while NFL owners decided which city should be awarded the second franchise. In the end, the owners voted 26-2 in favor of Jacksonville.

Chad Henne has been a quarterback for the Jacksonville Jaguars since 2012.

# JACKSONVILLE
# JAGUARS

**Stadium** EverBank Field

**Division** American Football Conference (AFC) South

**Head Coach** Gus Bradley

**Location** Jacksonville, Florida

**Super Bowl Titles** None

**Nicknames** Jags

## 6
### Playoff Appearances

## 7
### Winning Seasons

## 2
### Division Championships

# History

**HOT START**

The Jaguars reached the playoffs in **FOUR** of their first five seasons.

Tony Boselli was the Jaguars' first ever draft pick in 1995. In 2006, at the end of his professional career, Boselli signed a one-day contract with Jacksonville so he could retire as a Jaguar.

I n 1995, the Jacksonville Jaguars took the field for the first time. Under the guidance of head coach Tom Coughlin, players such as Mark Brunell, Tony Boselli, Jimmy Smith, and James Stewart treated Florida's football-hungry fans to some early success, with an impressive **winning percentage** for such a new team. They qualified for the 1996 AFC **playoffs** as a wildcard and traveled to Buffalo, New York, to face the heavily-favored Bills. Reserve running back Natrone Means exploded for 175 yards in a Jaguars upset win. A week later, against the number one Denver Broncos, Brunell, Keenan McCardell, Smith, and Means torched Denver's defense for 443 yards. The Jags' 30-27 victory was one of the biggest upsets in NFL playoff history.

In 1998, rookie running back Fred Taylor led the Jaguars to their first division title. The team won their second straight division title with a franchise-best 14 wins the following season. After a record-setting playoff win against the Miami Dolphins, the Tennessee Titans defeated the Jags. Under coach Jack Del Rio, the Jaguars returned to the playoffs in 2005 and 2007. Players such as Fred Taylor, Byron Leftwich, Maurice Jones-Drew, and David Garrard fueled an offense that posted an impressive playoff win against the Pittsburgh Steelers in 2007. Unfortunately, it was their last playoff win to date.

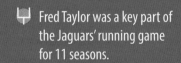 Fred Taylor was a key part of the Jaguars' running game for 11 seasons.

# The Stadium

EverBank Field seats 84,000 screaming fans.

The story of EverBank Field is one of renovation and renewal. Built on storied Florida football ground, EverBank stands on the site of Gator Bowl Stadium, home to the annual Gator Bowl game since 1946. While the original Gator Bowl Stadium underwent many renovations, pieces of that stadium were used in the construction of EverBank, giving it a physical link to the past.

Though the stadium's name has changed, Jaguars fans have only ever watched their team play on one field.

EverBank Field was originally known as Jacksonville Municipal Stadium. It was built to house the expansion Jacksonville Jaguars, as well as host the Gator Bowl and the annual game between the University of Florida and Georgia University. On February 6, 2005, the stadium hosted **Super Bowl** XXXIX. To prepare for the event, $47 million worth of renovations were made to the 10-year-old stadium. This included the addition of escalators and larger, wider video and scoreboards. In 2013, after two years of selling out every home game, Jacksonville's City Council approved a proposal to make $63 million worth of renovations to the stadium. New features will include the two largest video scoreboards in the world, platforms in the end zone areas with pools, and unique food items.

Hungry Jags fans look no further than Andrew Jackson's BBQ for delicious smoked pulled pork sandwiches.

# Where They Play

CANADA

Washington

30

Oregon

Montana

North Dakota

Idaho

South Dakota

Wyoming

Minnesota

*Lake Superior*

23 Wisconsin

22

Nevada

Utah

14

Nebraska

Iowa

24

13

Illinois

29

15

California

Colorado

Kansas

Missouri

31

UNITED STATES

16

Arizona

New Mexico

Oklahoma

Arkansas

32

Texas

17

Mississippi

*Pacific Ocean*

Louisiana

27

Alaska

Hawai'i

12

MEXICO

*Gulf of Mexico*

0  500 Miles
0  500 km

0  100 Miles
0  100 km

AMERICAN FOOTBALL CONFERENCE

| EAST | | NORTH | | SOUTH | | WEST | |
|---|---|---|---|---|---|---|---|
| 1 | Gillette Stadium | 5 | FirstEnergy Stadium | ★ 9 | EverBank Field | 13 | Arrowhead Stadium |
| 2 | MetLife Stadium | 6 | Heinz Field | 10 | LP Field | 14 | Sports Authority Field at Mile High |
| 3 | Ralph Wilson Stadium | 7 | M&T Bank Stadium | 11 | Lucas Oil Stadium | 15 | O.co Coliseum |
| 4 | Sun Life Stadium | 8 | Paul Brown Stadium | 12 | NRG Stadium | 16 | Qualcomm Stadium |

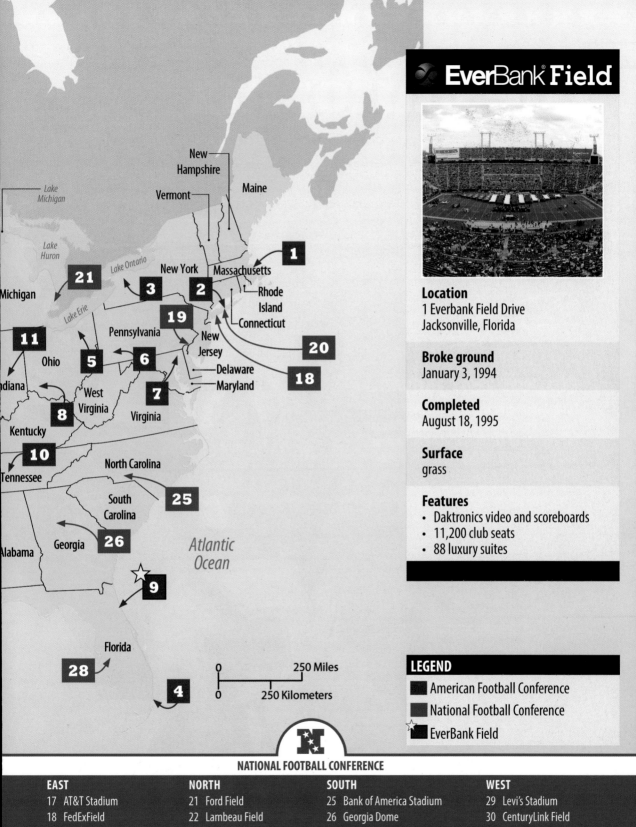

# EverBank Field

**Location**
1 Everbank Field Drive
Jacksonville, Florida

**Broke ground**
January 3, 1994

**Completed**
August 18, 1995

**Surface**
grass

**Features**
- Daktronics video and scoreboards
- 11,200 club seats
- 88 luxury suites

## LEGEND
- American Football Conference
- National Football Conference
- ☆ EverBank Field

## NATIONAL FOOTBALL CONFERENCE

| EAST | NORTH | SOUTH | WEST |
|------|-------|-------|------|
| 17 AT&T Stadium | 21 Ford Field | 25 Bank of America Stadium | 29 Levi's Stadium |
| 18 FedExField | 22 Lambeau Field | 26 Georgia Dome | 30 CenturyLink Field |
| 19 Lincoln Financial Field | 23 Mall of America Field | 27 Mercedes-Benz Superdome | 31 Edward Jones Dome |
| 20 MetLife Stadium | 24 Soldier Field | 28 Raymond James Stadium | 32 University of Phoenix Stadium |

# The Uniforms

## No, NOT *THAT* JAGUAR...

Ford Motor Company believed the original Jaguars logo looked a lot like their "Jaguar" car logo. The two sides worked out a deal, and the Jaguars football team changed their logo.

Paul Posluszny has not missed a game since he signed with Jacksonville, making all 32 starts during his two seasons as a Jaguar.

HOME

**B**efore the beginning of the 2013 season, the Jaguars unveiled new uniforms by Nike. The home jersey is black with white numerals outlined in teal and gold. The road jersey is white with teal numerals outlined in black and gold. The playoffs **alternate jerseys**, which are similar to the team's original jerseys, are teal with black numerals outlined in white and gold. All jerseys have a stripe that curves around the neck, as well as glossy patches on the shoulders resembling claw marks.

AWAY

For many years, the Jaguars wore white uniforms at home for the season's first eight games in order to stay cool in the sweltering Southern heat while their opponents roasted in dark jerseys.

NFL uniforms are designed to be lightweight and breathable, so players can make great plays, and celebrate, with ease.

# The Helmets

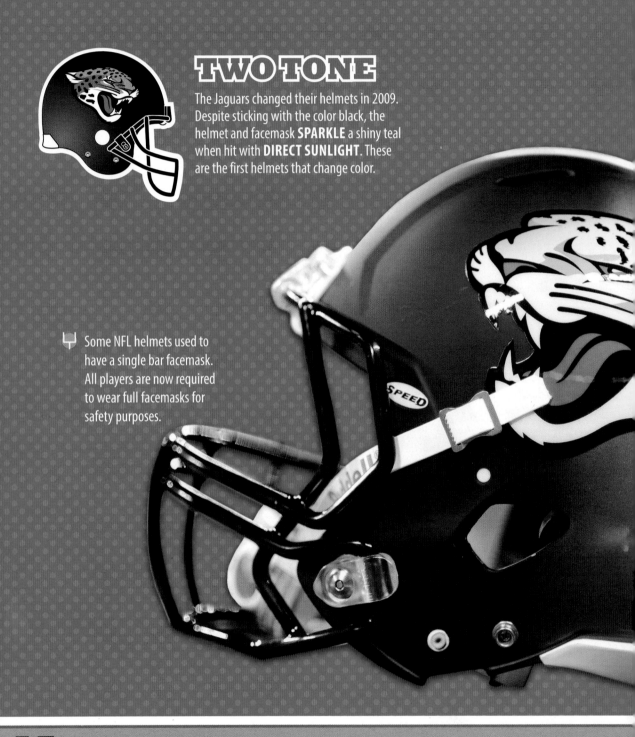

## TWO TONE

The Jaguars changed their helmets in 2009. Despite sticking with the color black, the helmet and facemask **SPARKLE** a shiny teal when hit with **DIRECT SUNLIGHT**. These are the first helmets that change color.

Some NFL helmets used to have a single bar facemask. All players are now required to wear full facemasks for safety purposes.

**F**rom 1995 through 2008, the Jacksonville Jaguars featured a black helmet with a blue facemask and a gold jaguar with a teal tongue. The design was considered to be one of the most creative in the NFL. In 2009, the team decided to make some improvements to the helmet color. Instead of plain black, the black was mixed with teal. The helmet came with a new facemask that was also metallic black teal.

In 2013, the Jaguars premiered their newest and boldest design, one that combined all the colors from the past and made slight alterations to the jaguar head. The new jaguar head is more realistic and features a fiercer-looking animal. Also, instead of merely having a teal tongue, teal has been added to its eyes and nostrils. The helmet's colors are now matte black and metallic gold, and the facemask is black.

Hits to the head are punishable in the NFL by penalty, fine, and even suspension.

# The Coaches

**4** Despite an 0-8 start to his head coaching career, Gus Bradley steadied his team and they won four of their next eight games, finishing with a 4-12 record.

With a winning percentage of 53.1 percent, Tom Coughlin is the most successful Jaguars head coach in the team's brief history.

**A** tradition of non-traditional head coaching was established in Jacksonville with the hiring of head coach Tom Coughlin in 1993. Jaguars' founder Wayne Weaver decided that the "intensity" of the candidate was more important than previous head-coaching experience. In their unconventional approach to staffing an expansion team, the Jaguars sped up their path to success.

### TOM COUGHLIN

Entering the 1995 season, the highest position Tom Coughlin had held in the NFL was wide receivers' coach. In eight years with the Jaguars, Coughlin coached the most successful expansion team in NFL history, qualifying for the playoffs four times and winning two division titles.

### JACK DEL RIO

In contrast to Coughlin's strict approach, Jack Del Rio was a player's coach. He made tight connections with his players and oversaw less difficult practices. Known as a defensive genius for his previous work in Baltimore and North Carolina, Del Rio coached the Jags to two playoff berths.

### GUS BRADLEY

In four years as Seattle's defensive coordinator, Gus Bradley transformed the Seahawk defense from 25th in the league to first. Having already enjoyed success at the college level and as an NFL linebackers' coach, his success came as no surprise. The 2013 Jaguars are a work in progress, but there is hope for the future.

# The Mascot

Jaxson de Ville certainly makes his entrance known as he sometimes bungee jumps off stadium lights and parachutes onto the field to announce his arrival.

**J**axson de Ville has been a steadfast presence on the Jacksonville Jaguars' sideline since 1996. Considered the team's "12th man," de Ville urges fans to cheer their hearts out and entertains them with daring feats and hilarious antics during breaks in the game.

Having worked tirelessly for 18 years, Jaxson de Ville is not the most modest of mascots. He recently branded himself "The Self-Proclaimed Best Mascot in Sports." However, his high opinion of himself is well deserved, as he has put up some eye-popping numbers over the years. He currently holds records for most pizzas eaten by a mascot during a single game, with 56, and highest rappel off a scoreboard, at 175 feet (53 meters).

Jaxson is very affectionate. In his 18 seasons with the Jaguars, he has hugged more than 250,000 fans.

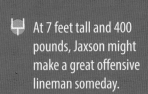
At 7 feet tall and 400 pounds, Jaxson might make a great offensive lineman someday.

# Legends of the Past

**M**any great players have suited up in the Jaguars' teal and gold. A few of them have become icons of the team and the city it represents.

## Tony Boselli

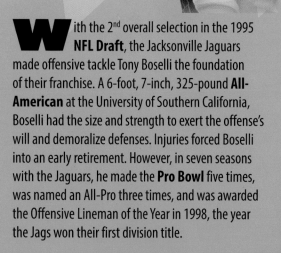

**Position** Offensive Tackle
**Seasons** 7 (1995–2002)
**Born** April 17, 1972, in Modesto, California

**W**ith the 2nd overall selection in the 1995 **NFL Draft**, the Jacksonville Jaguars made offensive tackle Tony Boselli the foundation of their franchise. A 6-foot, 7-inch, 325-pound **All-American** at the University of Southern California, Boselli had the size and strength to exert the offense's will and demoralize defenses. Injuries forced Boselli into an early retirement. However, in seven seasons with the Jaguars, he made the **Pro Bowl** five times, was named an All-Pro three times, and was awarded the Offensive Lineman of the Year in 1998, the year the Jags won their first division title.

## Fred Taylor

**F**ew running backs in the NFL have been as good for as long as Fred Taylor. Although he struggled to stay healthy during his first few seasons, Taylor was a reliable contributor, rushing for more than 1,000 yards seven times in 11 seasons as a Jaguar. In 2000, Taylor led the NFL in yards per game with 107.6. He established a career high of 1,572 rushing yards in 2003, while catching 48 passes out of the **backfield** for 370 yards. Despite all of his success, Taylor's lone appearance in the Pro Bowl came in 2007, a season in which he averaged an impressive 5.4 yards per carry.

**Position** Running Back
**Seasons** 13 (1998–2010)
**Born** January 27, 1976, in Pahokee, Florida

# Maurice Jones-Drew

**M**aurice Jones-Drew was a three-year starter for the University of California, Los Angeles Bruins. However, at five feet, eight inches and 205 pounds, many people thought that he was too small to succeed in the NFL. Jones-Drew did not waste much time proving his doubters wrong. In his rookie season, Jones-Drew rushed for nearly 1,000 yards, scored 16 touchdowns, averaged an incredible 5.7 yards per carry and racked up 2,250 **all-purpose yards**. The three-time Pro Bowler has since become a star, leading the NFL in rushing in 2011 and having a significant impact as a kick returner, receiver, and running back.

**Position** Running Back
**Seasons** 8 (2006–2013)
**Born** March 23, 1985, in Oakland, California

# Mark Brunell

**A**s Brett Favre's backup in Green Bay, Mark Brunell's opportunities to prove his worth on the field were limited. In 1995, the expansion Jaguars traded two draft picks for Brunell. In doing so, they sparked what would become the most successful run in NFL expansion history.

After taking over the starting role in 1995, Brunell led the Jags to a playoff berth in 1996, throwing for an NFL-best 4,367 yards. He would go on to lead the Jags to the playoffs three times in their first four years and make three Pro Bowls in the process.

**Position** Quarterback
**Seasons** 17 (1993–2011)
**Born** September 17, 1970, in Los Angeles, California

# Stars of Today

**T**oday's Jaguars team is made up of many young, talented players who have proven that they are among the best players in the league.

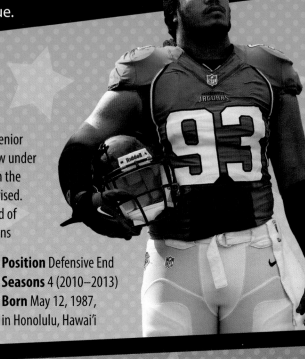

## Tyson Alualu

**D**espite being named first-team All-Pac-10 during his senior season at the University of California, Tyson Alualu flew under the NFL radar. When the Jacksonville Jaguars selected him with the 10th overall pick in the 2010 NFL Draft, many people were surprised. While he had great size and speed, he had not received the kind of national attention typical of a top 10 pick. In his first two seasons in Jacksonville, Alualu struggled with injuries. Despite concerns that he was not getting enough **sacks**, Alualu became a key run stopper on the Jaguars' defense. His size and speed requires the attention of two blockers, allowing the Jaguar linebackers to rush the passer.

**Position** Defensive End
**Seasons** 4 (2010–2013)
**Born** May 12, 1987, in Honolulu, Hawai'i

## Justin Blackmon

**A**s a wide receiver at Oklahoma State University, Justin Blackmon received national recognition. He won back-to-back Fred Biletnikoff Awards as the best wide receiver in the country and, after announcing his intentions to go pro, caught eight passes for 186 yards in a Fiesta Bowl victory. The Jaguars selected Blackmon with the fifth overall pick in the 2012 NFL Draft. In his rookie season, Blackmon led all NFL rookies with 64 receptions for 865 yards. In a single game against the Houston Texans, Blackmon had seven receptions for 236 yards.

**Position** Wide Receiver
**Seasons** 2 (2012–2013)
**Born** January 9, 1990, in Oceanside, California

# Paul Posluszny

**P**aul Posluszny, known by his teammates as "Poz," graduated from Pennsylvania State University as one of the most awarded linebackers in the school's storied history. As a linebacker for the Buffalo Bills, Poz quickly became the team's captain and defensive **most valuable player (MVP)**.

Since arriving in Jacksonville, Poz has led the team in tackles in three-straight seasons. In 2012, he set a franchise record with 139 tackles, while adding three interceptions, seven deflected passes, two sacks, and two forced fumbles.

**Position** Linebacker
**Seasons** 7 (2007–2013)
**Born** October 10, 1984, in Butler, Pennsylvania

# Josh Scobee

**S**ince 2004, the Jacksonville Jaguars have had the luxury of having one of the most reliable kickers in the NFL. Having only missed three in his career, Scobee ranks among the NFL's best **extra point** kickers, and he has ranked in the top three in touchbacks as well. The highlight of Scobee's career came in a Monday Night Football game against the Baltimore Ravens in 2012. In a defensive struggle, the Jags defeated the Ravens, 12-7. Scobee was good on all four of his field goal attempts, and tied an NFL record with three kicks of 50-plus yards in a single game.

**Position** Kicker
**Seasons** 10 (2004–2013)
**Born** June 23, 1982, in Longview, Texas

# All-Time Records

## 85.8 Career Passer-Rating

In nine seasons with the Jags, David Garrard was a model of consistency, limiting mistakes and completing a high percentage of his passes.

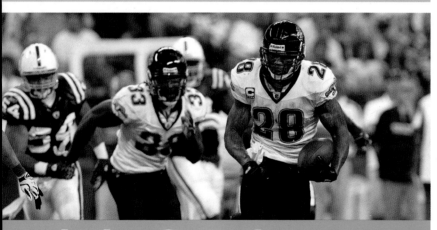

## 11,271 Career Rushing Yards

Fred Taylor rushed for more than 1,000 yards seven times in 11 seasons with the Jags.

# 1,606

### Single-season Rushing Yards

In 2011, Maurice Jones-Drew led the NFL in rushing yards and set the Jags' franchise mark.

# 25,698

## All-time Passing Yards

In eight years as the Jags' starting quarterback, Mark Brunell set the franchise record for passing yards.

# 12,287

### Career Receiving Yards

Mark Brunell's favorite target was Jimmy Smith. Smith amassed more than 1,000 receiving yards in nine seasons, including a streak of seven straight.

# Timeline

Throughout the team's history, the Jacksonville Jaguars have had many memorable events that have become defining moments for the team and its fans.

**1995**
In their **inaugural** season, the Jaguars look respectable, winning three of their first eight games. Mark Brunell starts 10 games at quarterback and, in his rookie season, Tony Boselli is a rock on the offensive line.

**January 4, 1997**
In one of the biggest upsets in NFL history, the second-year Jags travel to Denver and beat the top-seeded Broncos, 30-27. They return to Alltel Stadium early the next morning and discover 40,000 adoring fans there to greet them.

**January 15, 2000**
In the divisional round of the playoffs, the Jags blowout the Miami Dolphins, 62-7. Fred Taylor sets an NFL record with a 90-yard touchdown run and the Jacksonville defense forces seven turnovers. Sadly, the Jags lose to the Tennessee Titans for the third time that season in the AFC Championship Game.

| 1992 | 1994 | 1996 | 1998 | 2000 | 2002 |

**October, 1993**
Years of campaigning by an ownership group called "Touchdown, Jacksonville!" result in the NFL owners voting 26-2 to award the 30th NFL franchise to the city of Jacksonville. The vote is a surprise, as many football pundits expected the franchise to be awarded to Houston or Los Angeles.

*In 1999, the Jags ride the league's best defense to a franchise best 14-2 record and win their second straight division title.*

**1998**
In his rookie season, Fred Taylor amasses 1,644 **yards from scrimmage**, helping the Jags to another 11-win season and their first AFC Central crown.

**The Future**
After unprecedented early success, the Jaguars have endured some disappointing seasons. However, with young talent like Paul Posluszny and Tyson Alualu on the defensive side of the ball, the Jags are moving in the right direction. Gus Bradley has enjoyed tremendous success at every stop in his coaching career. After a somewhat rocky start, Jaguars fans remain hopeful that he will replicate that success in Jacksonville.

**2005**
Pro Bowl defensive tackles Marcus Stroud and John Henderson clog the middle, limiting the opposition's running game, and the Jags' defense carries them to a 12-4 record. Unfortunately, they finish behind the Indianapolis Colts and are forced to play a wild card game in New England, where they lose, 28-3.

On January 2, 2012, Shahid Khan purchases the Jags.

2004   2006   2008   2010   2012   2014

On January 5, 2008, in the Jags' first playoff win since January of 2000, they travel to Pittsburgh and defeat the Steelers.

**2003**
After three losing seasons, Jack Del Rio is named the Jags' new head coach. Fred Taylor rushes for career-high 1,572 yards and rookie quarterback Byron Leftwich replaces Mark Brunell as the team's starting quarterback.

**January 17, 2013**
After posting a franchise-worst 2-14 record in 2012, the Jags hire new head coach Gus Bradley. Maurice Jones-Drew returns from an injury that sidelined him much of the 2012 season, and although the Jags start the season 0-8, they begin to gel as a team, winning four of their next eight games.

# Write a Biography

## Life Story

A person's life story can be the subject of a book. This kind of book is called a biography. Biographies often describe the lives of people who have achieved great success. These people may be alive today, or they may have lived many years ago. Reading a biography can help you learn more about a great person.

## Get the Facts

Use this book, and research in the library and on the Internet, to find out more about your favorite Jaguar. Learn as much about this player as you can. What position does he play? What are his statistics in important categories? Has he set any records? Also, be sure to write down key events in the person's life. What was his childhood like? What has he accomplished off the field? Is there anything else that makes this person special or unusual?

## Use the Concept Web

A concept web is a useful research tool. Read the questions in the concept web on the following page. Answer the questions in your notebook. Your answers will help you write a biography.

# Concept Web

☐

**Adulthood**
- Where does this individual currently reside?
- Does he or she have a family?

☐

**Your Opinion**
- What did you learn from the books you read in your research?
- Would you suggest these books to others?
- Was anything missing from these books?

☐

**Childhood**
- Where and when was this person born?
- Describe his or her parents, siblings, and friends.
- Did this person grow up in unusual circumstances?

☐

**Accomplishments off the Field**
- What is this person's life's work?
- Has he or she received awards or recognition for accomplishments?
- How have this person's accomplishments served others?

## Write a Biography

☐

**Help and Obstacles**
- Did this individual have a positive attitude?
- Did he or she receive help from others?
- Did this person have a mentor?
- Did this person face any hardships?
- If so, how were the hardships overcome?

☐

**Accomplishments on the Field**
- What records does this person hold?
- What key games and plays have defined his or her career?
- What are his or her stats in categories important to his or her position?

☐

**Work and Preparation**
- What was this person's education?
- What was his or her work experience?
- How does this person work; what is the process he or she uses?

# Trivia Time

Take this quiz to test your knowledge of the Jacksonville Jaguars.
The answers are printed upside-down under each question.

**1** How many division championships have the Jacksonville Jaguars won since their beginning?

A. Two

**2** Which offensive lineman did the Jaguars select with their first ever draft pick?

A. Tony Boselli

**3** Who quarterbacked the Jaguars to their first playoff appearance?

A. Mark Brunell

**4** Who led the Jaguars in tackles in 2012?

A. Paul Posluszny

**5** What was the name of the organization responsible for bringing an NFL franchise to Jacksonville?

A. "Touchdown, Jacksonville!"

**6** Who holds the Jaguars' record for most all-purpose yards in a single season?

A. Maurice Jones-Drew

**7** Which Jacksonville running back set an NFL playoff record with his 90-yard touchdown run?

A. Fred Taylor

**8** What bowl game has the city of Jacksonville hosted since 1946?

A. The Gator Bowl

**9** Who is the Jaguars all-time leader in receptions and receiving yards?

A. Jimmy Smith

**10** Which rookie replaced Mark Brunell as the team's starting quarterback in 2003?

A. Byron Leftwich

# Key Words

**All-American:** a player, usually in high school or college, judged to be the best in each position of a sport

**all-purpose yards:** also referred to as combined net yards, all-purpose yards are a statistic that measures total yardage gained on receptions, runs from scrimmage, punt returns, and kickoff returns

**alternate jerseys:** a jersey that sports teams may wear in games instead of their home or away uniforms

**annual:** something that occurs once a year

**backfield:** the area of play behind either the offensive or defensive line

**expansion teams:** brand new teams in a sports league, usually from a city that has not hosted a team in that league before

**extra point:** an attempt awarded after each touchdown scored that allows the offensive team to kick the ball through the goalposts for an extra point

**Gator Bowl:** annual college football bowl game, a major post-season game between NCAA Division 1 teams

**inaugural:** marking the beginning of an institution, activity, or period of office

**most valuable player (MVP):** the player judged to be most valuable to his team's success

**NFL Draft:** an annual event where the NFL chooses college football players to be new team members

**playoffs:** the games played following the end of the regular season; six teams qualify: the four conference winners and the two best teams that did not finish first in their conference, called the wild cards

**Pro Bowl:** the annual all-star game for NFL players pitting the best players in the National Football Conference against the best players in the American Football Conference

**sacks:** a sack occurs when the quarterback is tackled behind the line of scrimmage before he can throw a forward pass

**Super Bowl:** the NFL's annual championship game between the winning team from the NFC and the winning team from the AFC

**winning percentage:** the number of games won divided by the total number of games played; a coach with 7 wins in 10 games would have a winning percentage of 70 percent

**yards from scrimmage:** the total of rushing yards and receiving yards from the yard-line on the field from which the play starts

FORT ZUMWALT WEST MIDDLE SCHOOL
150 WATERFORD CROSSING
O'FALLON, MO 63368-7135

# Index

# Log on to www.av2books.com

AV² by Weigl brings you media enhanced books that support active learning. Go to www.av2books.com, and enter the special code found on page 2 of this book. You will gain access to enriched and enhanced content that supplements and complements this book. Content includes video, audio, weblinks, quizzes, a slide show, and activities.

## AV² Online Navigation

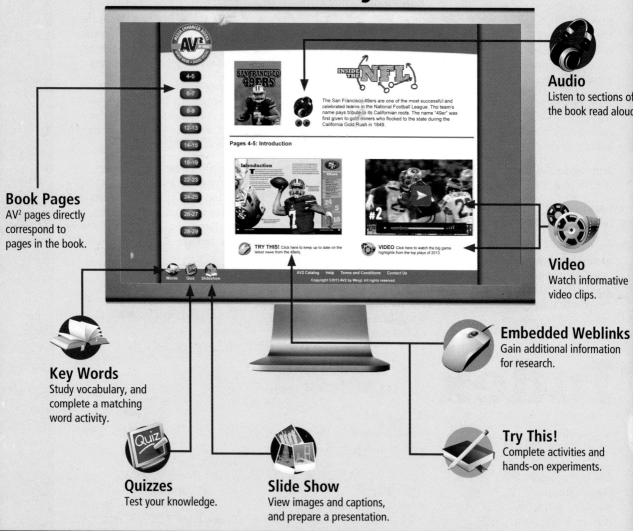

**Book Pages**
AV² pages directly correspond to pages in the book.

**Key Words**
Study vocabulary, and complete a matching word activity.

**Quizzes**
Test your knowledge.

**Slide Show**
View images and captions, and prepare a presentation.

**Audio**
Listen to sections of the book read aloud.

**Video**
Watch informative video clips.

**Embedded Weblinks**
Gain additional information for research.

**Try This!**
Complete activities and hands-on experiments.

AV² was built to bridge the gap between print and digital. We encourage you to tell us what you like and what you want to see in the future.

## Sign up to be an AV² Ambassador at www.av2books.com/ambassador.

Due to the dynamic nature of the Internet, some of the URLs and activities provided as part of AV² by Weigl may have changed or ceased to exist. AV² by Weigl accepts no responsibility for any such changes. All media enhanced books are regularly monitored to update addresses and sites in a timely manner. Contact AV² by Weigl at 1-866-649-3445 or av2books@weigl.com with any questions, comments, or feedback.